Taking Diabetes to School

by

Kim Gosselin

Published by
JayJo Books, LLC.
Valley Park, MO

<u>Taking Diabetes to School</u>

Copyright © 1998, by Kim Gosselin.

Second Edition. Third Printing. All rights reserved. No part of this book may be repro-
duced in any manner whatsoever without written permission form the publisher. For
information address JayJo Books, LLC., P.O. Box 213, Valley Park, MO 63088-0213.
Printed in the United States of America.

Published by
JayJo Books, LLC.
Publishing Special Books for Special Kids®
P.O. Box 213
Valley Park, MO 63088-0213

Library of Congress Cataloging-in-Publication Data
Gosselin, Kim
Taking Diabetes to School/Kim Gosselin - Second Edition - Third Printing
Library off Congress Catalog Card Number 97-76663
1. Juvenile/Non-Fiction
2. Health Education
3. Diabetes

ISBN 1 -891383-00-0
Library of Congress
First book in our *"Special Kids in School"®* series.

<u>**Taking Diabetes To School**</u> was formerly titled Jayson Goes To School -
Living With Diabetes in the Elementary School

Here's What Professionals Have to Say About
<u>Taking Diabetes to School</u>

<u>Taking Diabetes to School</u> is a superb children's book for kids with diabetes. This wonderfully illustrated book is written by a mother and her diabetic son, and will help children discuss their diabetes with their schoolmates and friends.

> Neil H. White, M.D.
> Associate Professor, Pediatrics,
> Washington University School of Medicine
> St. Louis Children's Hospital

Kim Gosselin has done a marvelous job of explaining the complexities of diabetes to young students in "kid" language! A **"MUST HAVE"** for every elementary school library!

> Connie Madigan, R.N., B.S.N.
> Elementary School Nurse

<u>Taking Diabetes to School</u> fills the enormous need of educating classmates of a child with diabetes. **A BARGAIN AT ANY PRICE!**

> Libby O'Connor, M.S.N., R.N., C.D.E. Manager,
> Diabetes Services Barnes Hospital, St. Louis, MO

<u>Taking Diabetes to School</u> offers sensitive insight into the day-to-day "school life" of a child with a chronic illness. Kim Gosselin has done an excellent job of conveying the message that a child with diabetes can live a happy, normal life! The "real" Jayson is a wonderful, happy, and talented little boy who is an inspiration to all who know and love him.

> Pat Thomas, M. Ed.
> Kindergarten Teacher, Living with Diabetes Herself.

More of What Professionals Have to Say About
Taking Diabetes to School

As a health care professional and mother, I found **Taking Diabetes to School** to be an insightful, poignant look into the school day of a child living with diabetes. **INSPIRATIONAL!!**

> Lynn Schratz, R.N., B.S.N.
> Clinical Research Specialist
> St. Louis University Hospital

Taking Diabetes to School is an easy to understand book written from the diabetic child's perspective. It SUPERBLY fills the very important need of educating teachers as well as classmates of young children living with diabetes.

> Anne Fitz, R.N., M.S.N.
> St. Louis Children's Hospital

An **EXCELLENT** idea! Does a wonderful job of educating kids with or without diabetes, and the illustrations are delightful!

> Jeanne Bubb, A.C.S.W., M.S.W. Diabetes Team
> Social Worker St. Louis Children's Hospital

Taking Diabetes to School was born out of necessity. It is education in the finest form and would have helped my own son tremendously when he was younger.

> Jackie Smith, Former NFL St. Louis Cardinal Football
> Player, and Father of a College Student Living with
> Diabetes.
> Member of the NFL Hall of Fame.

Acknowledgements

*With many thanks and true understanding
to all families living with diabetes.*

A portion of the sale of this book is donated specifically to help fund medical research and education. Thank you for your support.

All books published by JayJo Books, LLC. are available at special quantity discounts when purchased in bulk by corporations, organizations, or groups. Special imprints, messages, logos and excerpts can be produced to meet your needs. For more information, call (800) 801-0159.

Preface

On February 29, 1992, my son Jayson was diagnosed with Type I (insulin dependent) diabetes. It was just nine days after he celebrated his sixth birthday. Adjustments at home fell into place rather quickly. Injections, finger-pricks, and eating the proper foods were suddenly part of our regular routine. Attending school, however, presented a whole new set of frustrations and concerns. How could I expect Jayson's young classmates, or even his teachers to understand the complexities of diabetes?

Searching for a simple picture book on the topic of school and diabetes proved futile. I was appalled to find none available, and soon felt compelled to write one myself. Thus, **Taking Diabetes to School** was born! Since I began reading this little book to my son's classes, most of his "problems" regarding school and diabetes have been solved. His classmates have shown a new respect and admiration for Jayson. The children I have met delighted in the learning process and exhibited understanding and acceptance.

Taking Diabetes to School was designed to be read aloud in the child's classroom. Try to make it a fun event, and be prepared for some very bright questions from the other students! Involve your own child by asking him (or her) to pass out sugar-free treats when the story is finished. Of course, get permission from the teacher first!

Please feel free to write me in care of the publisher, as I welcome your comments and suggestions. My heart goes out to each and every one of you, and I yearn for the day when children no longer are **Taking Diabetes to School.**

Kim Gosselin

To my very special son Jayson,
whose courage and zest for life
continue to inspire me each and every day.

Hello boys and girls! My name is Jayson, and I'm a kid living with diabetes. Having diabetes means part of my body called the pancreas doesn't make enough insulin anymore. Because of this, I get too much sugar in my blood. Insulin is something special our bodies make to help turn sugar into energy. This sugar comes from the foods we eat.

Everyone has a pancreas, but not everyone gets diabetes.

Doctors and nurses don't know how or why I have diabetes. I didn't do anything wrong (like eat too many sweets), and it's **nobody's** fault! Doctors and nurses do know you can't catch diabetes from me. It's okay to play with me and be my friend.

I can't give you diabetes.

The only way for my body to get the insulin it needs now, is in a shot. Usually I get two or more shots each day. When I first went to the hospital, everyone did a great job of teaching me and my family about diabetes. We learned how to give shots at home. They don't hurt very much, and I can even do it myself (with help from my family, of course).

Getting a shot is just something I do everyday, like eating breakfast or brushing my teeth.

Because I have diabetes, it's important for me to eat healthy foods at about the same time each day. I follow a meal plan that I have written down. A meal plan works together with my insulin to help me stay healthy and feel my best. That means eating certain kinds of foods at special times during the day. It's a kind of "diet" that's good for anyone!

When you see me eating healthy snacks in class, it's because I'm following my meal plan.

To help keep my blood sugar in good control, I do a little blood test called a finger-prick. I have a small computer called a meter that tells me how much sugar is in my blood. This helps my doctors and nurses decide how much insulin my body needs. When you see me leave the classroom, I might be going to visit the school nurse. She helps me do a finger-prick. Teachers can help, too! When I'm at home, I usually do it myself.

The finger-prick test only takes a few seconds, and hardly even hurts.

Sometimes my blood sugar drops too low. This can happen if I exercise a lot, or don't have enough food in my body to balance my insulin. When I'm "low," I might act differently than I normally do. I might get shaky, hungry, or sleepy. At times I feel mean, angry, or confused. Please tell the teacher if you see me act this way. I need to eat or drink something with sugar in it **fast** when I'm feeling low. Orange juice or regular soda works great.

After a few minutes, I'll be back to my old self again!

Has anyone noticed the special bracelet I always wear? Bracelets aren't just for girls! Mine is really awesome! On the back it tells that I have diabetes. It also has a phone number to call in case of emergency (like if my blood sugar dropped too low, or if I had an accident). The people who answer the phone can tell the caller about diabetes and how to take special care of me.

I never take my bracelet off because someday it could save my life.

Like most kids, I love to play at recess and take part in gym class. I bet you do too! Unless I've just eaten a meal, it's probably best for me to have an extra snack before doing lots of exercise. Then I'm sure to have plenty of energy to play and have fun.

Diabetes doesn't stop me from doing anything other kids do!

I hope someday there will be a cure for diabetes. That means my doctors and nurses will be able to fix it! In fact, important people are working hard to find a cure every day. Until then, please don't treat me like I'm someone "different" because I have diabetes. After all, **nobody** is perfect!

I'm just Jayson; a kid living with diabetes, but a lot like **you** in every other way!

Let's Take The Diabetes Kids Quiz!

1. What is insulin?
Something special our bodies make to help turn the sugar in our foods into energy.

2. What part of my body doesn't make enough insulin anymore?
The pancreas.

3. Where in my body is the pancreas found?
Near my stomach.

4. Does someone get diabetes from eating too many sweets?
No!

5. Can you catch diabetes from me or anyone else?
No, so it's okay to play with me and be my friend.

6. Since my body doesn't make enough insulin anymore, how do I get the insulin my body needs?
I get my insulin in a shot, usually two or more each day.

Now turn the page to finish the quiz! ➔

7. Does getting your insulin shots hurt?
Not very much at all . . . I can even do it myself (with help from my family, my nurse, or my doctor, of course!)

8. What is a meal plan?
A meal plan is eating healthy foods at about the same time each day. It's important for me to stay on my meal plan. You may even see me eating snacks in class!

9. What is a finger-prick?
It's a simple blood test that tells me how much sugar is in my blood. This helps me know if I need to eat an extra snack sometimes or how much insulin my body needs.

10. What happens if my finger-prick blood test tells me my blood sugar is too low?
Then I need to eat or drink something with sugar in it FAST. Orange juice or regular soda works great!

Great Job! Thanks for taking the Diabetes Kids Quiz and learning more about Diabetes!

Ten Tips For Teachers

1. **EVERY CHILD LIVING WITH DIABETES IS DIFFERENT.**
   Each and every child living with diabetes may have different symptoms of "low" blood sugar. Although many of the symptoms may be similar, they will not always be the same. Situations that can affect your student's blood sugar are: insulin, food intake, exercise, illness, stress, and/or any changes in routine. Soon you will get to know your own student's unique individuality and their typical reactions to "low" blood sugar.

2. **DON'T DRAW UNNECESSARY ATTENTION TO YOUR STUDENT'S CONDITION.**
   Since your student living with diabetes may have to eat snacks periodically in the classroom, allow the whole class to have a snack at the necessary time. This tells the student who MUST have a snack that it's okay to eat when he or she needs to, without singling them out as being "different." In addition to your student's designated snack time, remember that he or she MUST eat whenever they feel "low." This is imperative, especially if the student is unable to have their blood sugar checked first by the school nurse. This is NOT a choice for the child living with diabetes, but a necessity!

3. **PROVIDE INCONSPICUOUS AND GENTLE REMINDERS.**
   Pay close attention to your student's regular snack time. Not all children (especially the very young) can tell time, or are going to remember their snack time. If you haven't noticed them eating, pass them a note or work out a special "password" between the two of you which reminds them of their snack time.

4. **DO NOT PUT A "LABEL" ON THE STUDENT LIVING WITH DIABETES.**
   Never single a child living with diabetes out as the "diabetic" kid. First and foremost, the child living with diabetes needs and wants to feel unique and special, just like every other student in your class.

5. **DO NOT SYMPATHIZE: EMPATHIZE.**
   A child with diabetes does not want or need your sympathy. These children need understanding, acceptance and support. Educate yourself in every way possible regarding Type I diabetes. Learn how it may affect them and have compassion for how they must live their lives each and every day.

6. **ALWAYS BE PREPARED.**
Always carry a quick and portable snack WHENEVER you and your student living with diabetes leave the classroom or the school grounds. This is especially important during fire drills, eathquake drills, field trips, special presentations, and/or assemblies. A small can of juice together with crackers may work best.

7. **USE THE BUDDY SYSTEM.**
If your student living with diabetes tells you he or she feels "low" and needs to see the nurse, ALWAYS send a "buddy" (someone who won't object) with them. In rare instances, the child's blood sugar may be so "low" that they may become disoriented and not make it to the nurse's office if left alone. Again, this is the rare extreme, but it does happen.

8. **ALLOW UNRESTRICTED BATHROOM BREAKS.**
When given the opportunity, let the child living with diabetes know that it's okay to go to the bathroom WHENEVER necessary. If their blood sugar is running "high," their body's natural response is to eliminate the extra glucose by using the bathroom. Don't make them feel embarrassed by having to ask you for permission.

9. **BE PATIENT.**
Be patient if the student living with diabetes has minor problems with organization. "High" and/or "low" blood sugar levels may make it difficult for them to concentrate at times. You may have to repeat some things, especially if they've been to the nurse's office during class time.

10. **KEEP THE LINES OF COMMUNICATION OPEN.**
Always work together with the student, caregivers, school nurse and other educators as a team player. If there is a special school party or occasion where "treats" are to be served, let the family know in advance, if possible. This allows the family to discuss the options with the child so that he or she can make responsible choices. Often, many "treats" can be worked into the child's regular meal plan.

To order additional copies of <u>Taking Diabetes to School</u> contact your local bookstore or library. Or call the publisher directly at (314) 861-1331. Please visit our website for further information and/or ordering information: **www.jayjo.com.** E-mail us at **jayjobooks@aol.com.**

Write to us at:
 JayJo Books, LLC.
 P.O. Box 213
 Valley Park, MO 63088-0213

Ask about our special quantity discounts for schools, hospitals, and affiliated organizations. Fax us at (314) 861-2411.

Look for other books by Kim Gosselin including:

From our *Special Kids in School*® series:
 <u>Taking Diabetes to School</u>
 <u>Taking Asthma to School</u>
 <u>Taking Seizure Disorders to School</u>
 And others coming soon!

Others Available Now!
 <u>SPORTSercise!</u>
 A "School" Story about
 Exercise-Induced Asthma
 <u>Taking Asthma to Camp</u>
 A Fictional Story about Asthma Camp
 <u>ZooAllergy</u>
 A Fun Story about Allergy
 and Asthma Triggers
 <u>Rufus Comes Home</u>
 Rufus The Bear With Diabetes™

<u>The ABC's of Asthma</u>
An Asthma Alphabet Book
for Kids of All Ages.
<u>Taming the Diabetes Dragon</u>
by Anne Dennis

and our first large hardcover book
<u>Smoking STINKS!!</u>™
From our new *Substance Free Kids*™ series.

Coming Fall '99
<u>Trick or Treat for Diabetes </u> <u>Taking A.D.D to School </u> <u>Taking Food Allergies to School</u>
by Kim Gosselin   by Ellen Weiner   by Ellen Weiner

A portion of the proceeds from all our publications is donated to various charities to help fund important medical research and education. We work hard to make a difference in the lives of children with chronic conditions and/or special needs. Thank you for your support.

Kim Gosselin

Kim Gosselin was born and raised in Michigan where she attended Central Michigan University. She began her professional writing career shortly after her two young sons were both diagnosed with chronic illnesses. Kim is extremely committed to bringing the young reader quality children's health education while raising important funds for medical research.

Kim now resides and writes in Missouri. She is an avid supporter of the Epilepsy Foundation of America, the American Lung Association, the American Cancer Society, and a member of the American Diabetes Association, the Juvenile Diabetes Foundation International, the society of Children's Book Writers and Illustrators, the Small Publishers Association of North America, the Publishers Marketing Association, and The Author's Guild.

Kim received the 1998 President's Award from the National Office of the American Lung Association for her work with chronically ill children and the 1998 National Female Family Friendly Business Award.